The Paradise Tree

Personal Prayer through Poetry

— J O H N D A V E Y —

Sacristy
Press

Sacristy Press
PO Box 612, Durham, DH1 9HT

www.sacristy.co.uk

First published in 2018 by Sacristy Press, Durham

Sacristy Limited, registered in England & Wales, number 7565667

British Library Cataloguing-in-Publication Data
A catalogue record for the book is available from the British Library

ISBN 978-1-910519-64-6

*I dedicate this book to Mary and to the parishioners
I have been privileged to serve, who have
journeyed with me on my pilgrimage of faith.*

Preface

This book is about personal discipleship and giving witness to the presence of God to the world around us. It is about finding within our inner being the meaning of life itself and about our future destiny. To do this we need to reflect upon the life and witness of a man who lived two thousand years ago and who, by his life of personal sacrifice to the needs of others in the name of love, gave visible expression to the reality and being of God, in the everyday life of humankind.

God is not someone somewhere out there in the vast expanse of the universe, but far closer to home; he is in our very heart and innermost being.

To Jesus Christ the key was given to open the portal to the secret garden of our longing, and that key was love. But his was no ordinary love; it was a sacrificial love that reunited us with our creator, into fellowship with our neighbour, and with all that was, is, and ever will be.

Contents

Introduction

Within the human psyche there is an innate spirituality, an awareness of another dimension to our being which has outwardly manifested itself in the form of numerous belief systems that have shaped human behaviour both beneficially and harmfully throughout history.

A common link between many of our world religions is the significance of the tree as a symbol of birth, death, and rebirth. The tree, with its branches reaching up into the sky and roots deep into the earth, can be seen to dwell in three worlds—heaven, earth, and the underworld. It is this powerful link between the Christian perception of the tree as a symbol of birth, death, and regeneration that has influenced the title of my book. In Genesis, we have the tree of knowledge and man's fall from grace. At Calvary, we have the tree of salvation, and, in the book of Revelation, the tree of life, a union of all being at one with God.

Our perception of the Christian God is based upon what we have been taught and what we have read for ourselves in the Bible. Belief in God and faith in God is commensurate with the fulfilment of our expectations of God. "Why should I believe in God? What has he done for me?" are questions that have a validity if we perceive God as an all-providing being who rewards and punishes according to merit. Who in their right mind would believe in an almighty being who lets his own beloved son die a horrible death on a cross, a God who says "suffer the little children to come unto me and woe betide those who harm them" and yet does nothing to prevent the death of innocent little ones in a mudslide or at the hands of a deranged gunman? Would you believe in a God who professes peace yet fails to prevent mass slaughter in wars and acts of terrorism? As for heaven and hell, can we really believe that such places exist? What of miracles, and the greatest miracle of all, resurrection from the dead? As for prayer, how many entreaties do we have to make before God does something to address our needs, wants, and desires? The answer to these questions lies within the depth of our own being.

"I am the light of the world," proclaimed Jesus of Nazareth, the son of a village carpenter, and the visible presence of God was revealed to humankind as a non-judgmental and self-giving God, who was loving, compassionate, and forgiving. Christ's teaching was simple to understand. It was about the awareness of our true identity as made in the image of God. Being a Christian is a call to give visible expression to his living presence in what we say and what we do in our time and to our generation. Believing in God is about believing in ourselves as made in God's image, and, as such, we become to the world around us his visible presence. As for prayer: all our prayers were answered when Jesus gave of himself to others in sacrificial love on the cross at Calvary.

The Word Made Flesh

The Bible is a record of man's perception of God through encounter with God. Written over time, the Bible encompasses every human emotion and places God at the heart of every human experience. At times, the Bible may baffle us with its contradictions, especially when it presents us with differing portrayals of God, ranging from cruel, indifferent, and revengeful, to caring, compassionate, forgiving, and nurturing. But it is a human record, and as such it reflects human nature and human need. Within the pages of the Old Testament, however, we discern, as through a veil, the shadow of the true God, a shadow that is given substance and reality in the humanity of God in the person of Jesus Christ. It has been said that we can only comprehend the Old Testament within the context of the New. The writer of Matthew's Gospel, for example, drew heavily upon scripture to win over his predominantly Jewish readers to the acceptance of Christ as the fulfilment of Messianic prophecy. A verse here and there, a prophecy, a story that has its parallel in the Gospels: all coming together to reveal the human face of God made manifest in his

Son, the living God. The Bible is timeless, but it needs to be understood in the context of our own time and our own situation. God speaks to us within the depths of our being with a contemporary voice. God is of the now. He is not history; he is an ever-present reality.

What is known about the life and witness of Jesus is to be found in the New Testament. The word "testament" is associated in legalistic terms with the last will and testament of a deceased person and the disposition of their assets, but it is more generally accepted by biblical scholars to mean the alliance (covenant) between God and Israel. St Paul uses this concept in the following passage from his first letter to the Corinthians, when he writes of the new covenant established by Jesus between God and man.

> For I received from the Lord what I also passed on to you: The Lord Jesus, on the night he was betrayed, took bread, and when he had given thanks, he broke it and said, "This is my body, which is for you; do this in remembrance of me." In the same way, after supper he took the cup, saying, "This cup is the new covenant in my blood; do this, whenever you drink it, in remembrance of me."
>
> *1 Corinthians 11:23–25*

The New Testament is made up of twenty-seven different books attributed to eight different authors, of whom six are numbered among the apostles (Matthew, John, Paul, James, Peter, and Jude) and two are disciples (Mark and Luke). The opening verses of the Gospel according to Luke give us an insight into how his life of Jesus came to be written.

> Many have undertaken to draw up an account of the things that have been fulfilled among us, just as they were handed down to us by those who from the first were eyewitnesses and servants of the word. With this in mind, since I myself have carefully investigated everything from the beginning, I too decided to write an orderly account for you, most excellent Theophilus, so that you may know the certainty of the things you have been taught.
>
> *Luke 1:1–4*

"The certainty of the things you have been taught" is a key phrase in understanding the reason for the differing accounts of the life of Jesus to be found in the New Testament. Each writer had a particular audience in mind, be it Jew, Greek, or Roman, and referenced the received wisdom of either Judaism, the philosophy of the classical world, or, as in the case of St Paul, Neoplatonism.

Of particular note in the first four books of the New Testament is the differing emphasis on the divinity of Jesus. Was this by birth or by endowment? Matthew and Luke begin with the birth of Jesus and the fulfilment of Messianic prophecy. The opening chapters of Mark and John, however, open with the baptism of Jesus and the descent of the Holy Spirit, an event that heralds the beginning of his ministry. The words of Jesus himself, however, make it quite clear that he believed that he was from the beginning at one with the being of God.

> Jesus replied, "If I glorify myself, my glory means nothing. My Father, whom you claim as your God, is the one who glorifies me. Though you do not know him, I know him. If I said I did not, I would be a liar like you, but I do know him and obey his word. Your father Abraham rejoiced at the thought of seeing my day; he saw it and was glad."
>
> "You are not yet fifty years old," they said to him, "and you have seen Abraham!"
>
> "Very truly I tell you," Jesus answered, "before Abraham was born, I am!"
>
> *John 8:54–58*

Theologians and biblical scholars have argued for centuries over the question of Christ's divinity, but this was not something that troubled Jesus himself. To his disciples at the Last Supper, Jesus said:

> The world cannot accept him [God the Father], because it neither sees him nor knows him. But you know him, for he lives with you and will

be in you. I will not leave you as orphans; I will come to you. Before long, the world will not see me anymore, but you will see me. Because I live, you also will live. On that day you will realize that I am in my Father, and you are in me, and I am in you.

John 14:17–20

The opening verses of John's Gospel mirror to some extent the opening words of Genesis, the first book of the Bible. They both begin with an account of the creation of life.

The Word Became Flesh

In the beginning was the Word, and the Word was with God, and the Word was God. He was with God in the beginning. Through him all things were made; without him nothing was made that has been made. In him was life, and that life was the light of all mankind.

John 1:1–4

In both Judaism and classical philosophy, *Logos* (word) is used to describe the active rational and spiritual principle that permeates all reality. In John's Gospel, Jesus is identified as God revealing himself to the world. Jesus as Logos, the word incarnate, is God in self-revelation and in redemptive life. Illumination is the creative dynamic that brings forth reality; Jesus declared: "I am the light of the world."

Creation myths abound in the development of human society; at first passed on from generation to succeeding generation by word of mouth, they later became enshrined in literature, as in the case of the Bible. Myths like the parable stories of Jesus convey profound truths and should not be interpreted historically or literally. Their imagery gives insight into the comprehension of our being in relation to the world around us. Belief in a creator being who brings order out of chaos, light out of darkness, and the very breath of life itself to all being, is conveyed very well in the following passage from the Book of Proverbs, a lesson set for Trinity Sunday in the Christian calendar.

> The Lord brought me forth as the first of his works,
>> before his deeds of old;
> I was formed long ages ago,
>> at the very beginning, when the world came to be.
> When there were no watery depths, I was given birth,
>> when there were no springs
>> overflowing with water;
> before the mountains were settled in place,
>> before the hills, I was given birth,
> before he made the world or its fields
>> or any of the dust of the earth.

I was there when he set the heavens in place,
   when he marked out the horizon
   on the face of the deep,
when he established the clouds above
   and fixed securely the fountains of the deep,
when he gave the sea its boundary
   so the waters would not overstep his command,
and when he marked out the foundations of the earth.
   Then I was constantly at his side.
I was filled with delight day after day,
   rejoicing always in his presence,
rejoicing in his whole world
   and delighting in mankind.

Proverbs 8:22–31

As the frontiers of science expand to the stars and beyond, ascribing creation to a supreme being becomes less and less credible to our generation, but God's creation is not about matter; it is about birth and concept. The breath of God as the formative essence of our being lies at the heart of the Christian Gospel, and nowhere is this more clearly stated than in the following passage from John.

God is spirit, and his worshipers must worship
in the Spirit and in truth.

John 4:24

The Light

On earth the sea doth ebb and flow
To pull of sun and moon,
And jewels of past and present light,
As stars above, are strewn.

The alpha and the omega,
Beginning and world's end;
From dust we came, to dust return,
And thence to heaven ascend.

For days of man are but as grass
To flourish and to fade,
And like the sun return to dust,
From which all things are made.

But look you to the ray of light
In which we dance and play,
Its warmth the touch of love divine;
Rejoice and seize the day.

Science has opened the door to reveal the wonder of creation from its first beginning, but there is a mystery yet to be discovered about humankind. The Bible gives this mystery a name: the breath of God. It is the breath of creative energy that inspires the artist, the writer, and the composer, and it comes from within. The conception process may be explained scientifically in terms of brain activity in the frontal lobe, but the mystery still remains, and that is as it should be.

Conception has both a physical and spiritual dimension, and this is evident in the pages of the Bible, in the stories of both the birth of Jesus and his baptism. In the renaissance period, a popular subject for artists was St Anne teaching Mary to read. Human behaviour may be attributed to the twin forces of nature and nurture, each of which has equal validity, but whether behavioural outcomes are dependent on our DNA, more than, say, life experiences and our environment, is still very much open to debate.

In my own case, Christian nurture, I am sure, played a significant part in my calling to the priesthood.

I was born five years before the outbreak of the Second World War, and my earliest memory is of being evacuated from London at the age of four to St Ives, a market town in Huntingdonshire, where I was billeted with the spinster daughter of a non-conformist minister. On Sunday mornings I attended Chapel, and on Sunday afternoons, toys were put away and stories from the

Bible were read to me. Sunday worship became part of my life as I grew to maturity.

The devout parents of Jesus religiously observed the customs and rites of their faith, presenting him to the Lord, as prescribed by the law, and making their yearly pilgrimage to the Temple in Jerusalem. A visit to Jerusalem at the age of twelve is recorded in the second chapter of Luke; during the visit, Jesus was discovered after a lengthy search to be sitting with the teachers and putting questions to them. In the Gospels, Jesus is addressed by his followers as Rabbi, signifying one who was well versed in Judaic law, writings, and prophecies.

> [Jesus] went to Nazareth, where he had been brought up, and on the Sabbath day he went into the synagogue, as was his custom. He stood up to read, and the scroll of the prophet Isaiah was handed to him. Unrolling it, he found the place where it is written:
> "The Spirit of the Lord is on me,
>   because he has anointed me
>   to proclaim good news to the poor.
> He has sent me to proclaim freedom for the prisoners
>   and recovery of sight for the blind,
> to set the oppressed free,
>   to proclaim the year of the Lord's favour."
>
> Then he rolled up the scroll, gave it back to the attendant and sat down. The eyes of everyone in

the synagogue were fastened on him. He began by saying to them, "Today this scripture is fulfilled in your hearing."

All spoke well of him and were amazed at the gracious words that came from his lips. "Isn't this Joseph's son?" they asked.

Luke 4:16–22

The Word Made Flesh

When Anne taught Mary how to read,
God's word became a ripening seed
That in her virgin womb gave birth
To Christ Incarnate, here on earth.

From prophecy a cloth we weave
To bind our faith and child conceive
From Spirit and the will of mind,
"At one" with God, in humankind.

The Holy Books, both old and new,
Enwrap the flesh of what is true:
The secret of God's plan for man,
His purpose since the world began.

The gospel stories Christ proclaim,
And we, who bear His holy name,
God's presence here on earth should be:
The word made flesh for all to see.

The Tree of Life

The desire for personal identity and self-realisation is innate in humankind as is the quest for knowledge and greater understanding of the world around us. We are explorers and innovators, striving to push the boundaries and to reach out to the universe beyond planet earth. But at the same time there is an awareness of loss. The price to be paid for knowledge is guilt, and yet we are unable to articulate the precise nature of our dis-ease. Paradise is described in the book of Genesis as a garden where all is in harmony and God walks with man, but tasting the fruit of knowledge brought discord. It is not what we know but how we use the knowledge we have acquired that can spell disaster and disquietude for the human spirit. As a child returning to London after the war, I played in the ruins of a city where human habitations had been reduced to rubble. Enduring memories for me are the newsreel footage of the aftermath of the dropping of the atomic bombs on Hiroshima and Nagasaki and the scenes of unspeakable horror revealed to the world in newsreel footage when the Allies liberated the Nazi concentration camps.

For the word of God is alive and active. Sharper than any double-edged sword, it penetrates even to dividing soul and spirit, joints and marrow; it judges the thoughts and attitudes of the heart. Nothing in all creation is hidden from God's sight. Everything is uncovered and laid bare before the eyes of him to whom we must give account.

Hebrews 4:12–13

The Paradise Tree (1)

When God created humankind
And all the world was of one mind,
There was a garden with a tree,
Its fruit forbidden by decree.

The crop it bore, for good or ill,
Was knowledge of one's own freewill.
Temptation's coil enwrapped poor Eve,
And sought with wisdom to deceive.

But God knows all that is, and reads
Our inner thoughts that maketh deeds.
We cannot cloak our nakedness,
Nor hide our inner wickedness.

When we forego our innocence,
With nought to say in our defence,
The price is banishment and shame,
Forever seeking whence we came.

The Paradise Tree (2)

Lost Souls, we wander in the maze
Of free will's labyrinthine ways,
But God had pity on our plight;
And sent his Son to set us right.

And on the hill of Calvary
God gave to man another tree;
The fruit it bore, for all to find,
Redeeming love in will and mind.

For, from the cross, new life did spring,
And hope became a living thing:
Forgiveness for man's fall from grace,
And freedom from sin's coiled embrace.

The Cross a sign for all to see,
And writ thereon, "Come. Follow me."
For here begins the journey home,
To paradise, from whence we came.

What has been lost in man's quest for knowledge is the true nature of creative, self-giving love. In the above two poems I have linked the paradise tree in the Garden of Eden with the tree planted by God at Calvary.

There is reference in the Book of Revelation to another tree, planted by God beside the river in the kingdom of heaven, and this is the tree of life.

> Then the angel showed me the river of the water of life, as clear as crystal, flowing from the throne of God and of the Lamb down the middle of the great street of the city. On each side of the river stood the tree of life, bearing twelve crops of fruit, yielding its fruit every month. And the leaves of the tree are for the healing of the nations. No longer will there be any curse. The throne of God and of the Lamb will be in the city, and his servants will serve him. They will see his face, and his name will be on their foreheads. There will be no more night. They will not need the light of a lamp or the light of the sun, for the Lord God will give them light. And they will reign for ever and ever.
>
> *Revelation 22:1–5*

Shortly after my appointment as Chaplain and Minor Canon, I was called upon to deliver a sermon in the presence of Her Majesty the Queen and eighteen Anglican bishops in St George's Chapel, Windsor Castle. My text

was from Genesis 28:10–20, Jacob's dream in which
he saw a stairway to heaven and angels ascending and
descending.

> When Jacob awoke from his sleep, he thought,
> "Surely the Lord is in this place, and I was not
> aware of it." He was afraid and said, "How
> awesome is this place! This is none other than
> the house of God; this is the gate of heaven."
>
> *Genesis 28:16–17*

I proceeded with caution to suggest that Jacob's dream
was a vision of the true heaven here on earth.

The Stairway to Heaven

The Genesis of life on earth
And mystery to man,
The answer sought from heaven above,
In space where all began.

Up thrusting from this planet earth,
Man's quest to reach the stars,
A stairway to explore new worlds,
And sign of life on Mars.

But Jacob had another dream,
And saw creation's hand
Not high above this world of ours,
But coming down to land.

A ladder twixt two worlds as one,
Where dream and will accord,
And we become creation's space,
Indwelling for God's Word.

Our lives have a beginning and an end, and our journey through life is one of growth, discovery, challenge, heartaches, and joy. The labyrinth is held to be symbolic of our journey through life and the decisions we have to make on the way. In recent times, labyrinths have been constructed in many Christian communities as an aid to meditative prayer, signifying the journey of the soul to the within-ness of our being.

The thread of Ariadne ("purity" in Cretan Greek) guided Theseus out of the labyrinth, and, in Plato's dialogue, Socrates uses this metaphor with telling effect.

> Then it seemed like falling into a labyrinth: we thought we were at the finish, but our way bent round and we found ourselves as it were back at the beginning, and just as far from that which we were seeking at first. … Thus the present-day notion of a labyrinth as a place where one can lose one's way must be set aside. It is a confusing path, hard to follow without a thread, but, provided [the pilgrim] is not devoured at the midpoint, it leads surely, despite twists and turns, back to the beginning.
>
> **Socrates, in Plato's Euthydemos**

The life and witness of Jesus Christ, the Alpha and Omega, the beginning and the end, is the thread that will guide us back to paradise, to that eternity of being that is God, the divine Logos, word made flesh.

The Soul of Man

Then the Lord God formed a man from the dust
of the ground and breathed into his nostrils the
breath of life, and the man became a living being.

Genesis 2:7

The breath of life is the soul of man. It is the source of
one's physical and psychological nature and is linked to
both instinctive and learned behavioural responses to
internal and external stimuli. That part of the soul we
term the human spirit is associated with moral virtues
and the ability to distinguish between good and evil. It
is the human spirit that separates man from all other
creatures. It is related to the intellect and allows us to
have an awareness of the otherness of our being and our
relationship with the divine order.

Then he said to them all: "Whoever wants to be
my disciple must deny themselves and take up
their cross daily and follow me. For whoever
wants to save their life will lose it, but whoever
loses their life for me will save it. What good

is it for someone to gain the whole world, and yet lose or forfeit their very self? Whoever is ashamed of me and my words, the Son of Man will be ashamed of them when he comes in his glory and in the glory of the Father and of the holy angels.

"Truly I tell you, some who are standing here will not taste death before they see the kingdom of God."

Luke 9:23–27

"Take up your cross" is the point of commitment in faith when we as individuals make the life-changing decision to put our trust in God.

Take Up Your Cross

Can you not see what I can see?
A world for humankind,
Where love and truth go hand in hand,
A world for you to find.

A world where wars have ceased to be,
And wolf lies down with lamb,
Where we exist in harmony,
With nature, race and clan.

To seek this world, take up your cross
And follow where it leads.
Fear not the journey, nor the cost,
For Christ will meet your needs.

And though the way be hard and long,
You'll never be alone,
For Christ will take you by the hand,
To guide you safely home.

The "He" in Me

For many, the image persists of God as an omniscient being who resides beyond the clouds, presiding over a court of judgement and retribution. But the truth, revealed to the world in the words and witness of Jesus Christ, is that God is the spirit and the breath of our being. The words of Jesus to the Samaritan woman provide us with an insight into how he understood the nature and being of God.

> Yet a time is coming and has now come when the true worshipers will worship the Father in the Spirit and in truth, for they are the kind of worshipers the Father seeks. God is spirit, and his worshipers must worship in the Spirit and in truth."
>
> The woman said, "I know that Messiah" (called Christ) "is coming. When he comes, he will explain everything to us."
>
> Then Jesus declared, "I, the one speaking to you—I am he."
>
> *John 4:23–26*

The breath of God is the creative gift of God, and the Spirit of God is the image of God, the substance and being of God, revealed to the world by the acts of God that bear witness to his presence.

Witness and discipleship are the key words in Christianity. They are the bedrock on which the fellowship of believers has been founded. But the Church, the Body of Christ, is not a building as was the Temple in Jerusalem; it is a living, breathing revelation of the presence of God in all that is done to alleviate the suffering and needs of humanity in his name.

Therefore, as God's chosen people, holy and dearly loved, clothe yourselves with compassion, kindness, humility, gentleness and patience. Bear with each other and forgive one another if any of you has a grievance against someone. Forgive as the Lord forgave you. And over all these virtues put on love, which binds them all together in perfect unity.

Let the peace of Christ rule in your hearts, since as members of one body you were called to peace.

Colossians 3:12–15

Then Jesus came to them and said, "All authority in heaven and on earth has been given to me. Therefore go and make disciples of all nations, baptizing them in the name of the Father and of the Son and of the Holy Spirit, and teaching them to obey everything I have commanded you. And surely I am with you always, to the very end of the age.

Matthew 28:18–20

The Spirit

The Spirit is the seed of God;
The Spirit is the soul of man.
The Spirit is the breath of life,
Creator when God's world began.

The Spirit is the light of God;
The Spirit is a Holy flame.
The Spirit is the torch of God,
That lightens darkness in His name.

The Spirit is a hurricane;
The Spirit is a mighty wind.
The Spirit is the still, small voice
That speaks a tongue I comprehend.

The Spirit is the prophet's dream,
The Spirit He who can fulfil.
The Spirit is the driving force
That gives me strength to do God's will.

Reflections

Sacred verse inspired by passages from the Bible

St Paul's encounter with Christ on the Damascus road was for him a "Eureka" moment of revelation and illumination. The veil of the Old Covenant had been lifted and he beheld the true face of God. In his second letter to the Corinthians, Paul writes:

> But whenever anyone turns to the Lord, the veil is taken away. Now the Lord is the Spirit, and where the Spirit of the Lord is, there is freedom. And we all, who with unveiled faces contemplate the Lord's glory, are being transformed into his image with ever-increasing glory, which comes from the Lord, who is the Spirit.
>
> **2 Corinthians 3:16–20**

BETHLEHEM BOUND

Advent

The night descends,
And silence drifts through ancient quires
To still the earnest voice,
The beating wing of music's golden flight.
Exploring rays of moonlight scan
Grey medieval walls,
Illuming ghosts from ancient dreams.
Fantastic masks, lewd images of fear,
Glare balefully upon the counterpoise
Of heaven's angel host
With trumpets poised
To sound a fanfare
For the coming of the Lord.
Beyond the shadow nave
The Eagle stands,
Upon whose mute supporting wings,
The chronicle of life immortal waits
To greet the Advent dawn.

The Annunciation

Inspired by Luke 1:26–38

Behold a virgin shall conceive,
And man shall see God face to face.
A promise made, and now fulfilled,
To manifest His saving grace.

How blessed am I that God has deigned
To dwell within my human heart,
To share my life and be with me
And of His love make me a part.

The Visitation

Inspired by Luke 1:39–45

A burden, yet no cause for shame;
And to Elizabeth I came,
To share with her the joyful news
That he a humble maid did choose
To bring to birth His only Son,
And show the world that God is come.

Mary's Lullaby

O Holy babe of Bethlehem,
New life and love of God to bring,
You slumber now in sweet repose,
While all around you angels sing.

When you awake, O Holy Child,
Grant me the strength to succour thee,
To hold you in my arms of love,
And dry the tears you shed for me.

Nativity

A promise made and now fulfilled,
"Salvation come", as God has willed.

The crib a sign of man's new birth
And God come down from heaven to earth.
The cross a sign of sins forgiven
And man at one with God in heaven.

Prayer

Lord, grant me eyes to see as thee,
The faith to know the "thee" in me,
The strength to act as you would do,
And will to live my life for you.

Joseph

Inspired by Matthew 1:18–25

A piece of wood I understand,
And fashion it by eye and hand.
But she, with child, perplexes me,
I knew her not. How can this be?
To break the troth betwixt us made
Would bring down shame and her degrade,
And this, for love, I'd never do;
O Lord, I place my trust in you.
And in a dream the voice of love
Assurance gave from heaven above;
"Fear not this blessed maid to wed,
The child she bears," the Spirit said,
"Is God's own son, Emmanuel,
That He, with you, may come to dwell."
In Bethlehem the babe was born,
To worship him were shepherds drawn,
And wise men from afar came there,
With gold and frankincense and myrrh.
But, warned of Herod's vile intent,
Another way they homeward went,
And I by angels told to flee
To Egypt with my family.

Simeon

Inspired by Luke 2:25–32

A lifetime spent in earnest quest:
An old man's dream of peace at last;
For here, within my arms I hold
The one whose coming was foretold.
The light to shine for humankind,
For all who seek to surely find
The truth that God dwells in our heart,
And in our hands ere we depart.

Anna

Lord, how I longed to see your face,
And feel the warmth of your embrace.
A woman called by God to be
His human voice in prophecy,
I knew at once that it was you,
The Saviour here, and all is true.
At eighty-four my days are done,
But yours, sweet child, have just begun.
You will return, of this I'm sure;
Your voice be heard for evermore.

Bright Was the Star

Bright was the star
In the eastern sky,
The birth of the Christ-child,
In Bethlehem nigh.
The seekers for truth
Travelled far to behold
The wonder revealed,
Much brighter than gold,
The Light that shone
From a human face,
When lit from within
By God's loving grace.

THE COMING OF CHRIST

On Jordan's Bank

Inspired by Matthew 3:11–17

"Repent. Repent," the Baptist cried,
And people came from far and wide
To hear the herald of God's word
Proclaim the coming of the Lord.

Make straight the path, the way prepare,
Repentance prove by fruit you bear.
For lo, He comes new life to bring
To all who turn away from sin.

The Harbinger

He came like me, an infant out of time;
His mother but a child herself,
And mine well past her fruitful prime.
A promise made, a prophecy fulfil,
And I, the harbinger of grace
As God didst will.
Though close of kin,
We chose to go our separate ways.
I turned my back upon this world of sin
But he, a social man
(A drunkard and a glutton some did say),
Befriended all, and sought their souls to win.
And when he came
To be baptized of me
The signs were there:
The dove,
God's portent from above
And voice which spoke
Approval of His Son.
The message I proclaimed
Was now become reality.
My work was done.

Repentance was my theme;
And cleansing did I give from earthly sin,
But He, the Holy Spirit and eternal life—
Creations new beginning from within;
I hear by good report the lame do walk,
The blind receive their sight;
And much else does he do
Of which they talk.
I wait the fate of death;
And so does He.
But by His death
Is promise of eternal life for me.

The Temptation

Inspired by Matthew 4:1–11

Christ shunned the glory of this present age
And sought the solace of a desert place,
To find the presence of the living God
And wait upon the Holy Spirit's grace.

O how I hunger for that living bread,
The word made flesh that He alone can give.
No other food can feed my inmost soul
And by God's grace grant Christ in me to live.

Though tempted as he was, Christ did not fall,
For God upholds his children from within.
O Spirit of the Lord, hold fast to me,
Lest I be tempted to succumb to sin.

The kingdoms of this world were naught to Him;
Self-glory he decried though he a King.
He came to serve his blessed father's will,
And to the world a holy kingdom bring.

A Marriage in Cana

Inspired by John 2:1–11

A marriage feast, a mother's plea
That water might be turned to wine.
"Would not my son do this for me?"
But now was not the place or time.

But this, perhaps, the time to show
The fullness of God's saving grace,
By turning water into wine
And cleanse from sin the human race.

And when, at supper with his friends,
Our Lord took wine to share with them,
This sign a sacrament became,
That we might be at one with him.

When Jesus taught his followers
New wine must in new vessels be,
The blood he shed upon the cross,
New wine, new life, he gave to me.

Follow Me

Andrew, Peter, James and John,
Fishermen of Galilee,
Left their nets to follow him,
When the Lord said "Come with me."

After he had prayed all night
For the Father's guiding hand,
Christ chose twelve to follow him
And become his faithful band.

Christ's Apostle we must be:
To the world His words proclaim;
Heal the sick; support the weak;
Feed the hungry in His name.

Awesome is the thought that He
Chose to place his faith in me,
To proclaim His living word
And on earth His presence be.

Faith

Inspired by Matthew 14:25–33

I had a dream that I could fly.
If only dreams like this were true;
A dove I'd be, and soar up high
To seek another world for you.
But reason and reality
Have clipped my phantom wing,
And to this ark, this mortal me,
This earth-bound world, I cling.
A dream is like a seed, they say,
And we the soil to make it grow;
But there is something else I need:
The will and faith to make it so.
I saw him walk upon the sea.
I thought I too could do the same;
But courage failed me when I tried,
And to my rescue Jesus came.
I shared his dream to save the world;
And dreams are father to the deed.
He taught that mountains could be moved,
And by such faith we would succeed.

The Transfiguration

Inspired by Luke 9:28–36

Transfigured by the light that shone
All glorious like sun on snow,
His clothing shimmered like a jewel;
And face afire with heavenly glow.

I only once have seen this light
Upon the face of humankind,
And this from love's true innocence,
With uncorrupted heart and mind.

"This is my Son, my chosen one,"
I heard a voice from heaven say.
The cloud that had obscured my ken
Was lifted from my mind that day.

The mountaintop, a refuge from
The darkness of the world below;
But to the world He did return,
And on mankind His light bestow.

The mountaintop: a place for meditation, prayer, and transfiguration, where all notions of self are dispelled, and one becomes in union with all that was, is, and can be; a place of inner illumination and understanding. The mystic is not the ascetic with his or her head in the clouds, but one who understands that a deeper knowledge of the divine purpose of creation brings one to a much richer involvement in this world, for it is specifically in this world that one can make a dwelling for the creator who desires to have an abode within our being.

Beatitude

How blessed are they who come to me,
The kingdom of the Lord they'll see;
Though poor, they'll want not nor be sad,
For I shall make their hearts be glad.

The meek shall overcome the strong,
And to the humble, earth belong.
All those who hunger will be fed
By God's own hand, with his blessed bread.

All those who from their hearts forgive,
Forgiveness will themselves receive.
The pure in heart will see God's face,
And stand before his throne of grace.

For saints above and here below,
Who serve the Lord and grace bestow,
All glory and due praise we give;
They, in our hearts, shall ever live.

HEALING GRACE

~

A Mother's Plea

Inspired by Matthew 15:22–28

Would he not heed a mother's plea?
To grant a daughter pain's release,
Bring healing to a troubled mind,
And hear my prayer at very least.

Did he not say "Go, seek the lost,
Bring sheep from other folds to me"?
To save the world, God sent his son;
I am the world, could he not see?

Though God had chosen Abraham
And all descendants of his race,
Each one of us is rightful heir
And worthy of God's saving grace.

The crumbs that fall would he deny
To those who hunger for that bread,
The manna of eternal life,
Which cometh from God's table spread?

Did Christ not say, upon the Mount,
"All those who ask, they shall receive;
And those that seek shall surely find"?
The words he spoke one should believe.

Persistence has its own reward;
I plead again; he answered me,
"Your daughter shall this day be cured."
My faith in him had set her free.

Feeding the Multitude

In serried ranks, we listened
To his honeyed words:
Such wisdom
From a man we knew so well.
Four thousand strong,
An army hungry for a fight.
Could this be He,
The promised one,
To lead us on to victory?
But what he preached
Was not a call to arms;
He spoke of love for fellow man, not war.
And he with broken bread
Another hunger met.
The hope that we
Might be as one
The "He in us"
For all the world to see.

Bethesda

Inspired by John 5:2–9

They said he would be passing by
But would he hear my feeble cry?
The others, when the waters stir,
Press forward and my place deny.

For eight and thirty years had I
Been waiting for a helping hand,
To take me to Bethesda's pool,
For by myself I could not stand.

Such was my fate. But then I sensed
A shadow hover over me,
"Take up your bed and walk," he said.
Would this were true. It cannot be.

But when he questioned my desire
To be made whole, and took my hand,
My strength I felt restored to me,
And rise I did at his command.

Sight of Mind

Inspired by John 9:1–5

There was no dawn,
No benediction in the sun's
Dispelling of the dark for me.
These eyes of mine
Reflected not the beauty
Of its roseate blush,
For I was blind!
Until he came with radiant light,
And I at last could see.

Blindness is interpreted as a metaphor for our inability to see the coming of the "Light" (of Christ).

Redemption

I curl myself into a ball
And make believe that I am small:
Once more a child of innocence.
But ignorance is no defence;
No excuses then for me,
And I must face reality.
A lifetime spent in sad regret,
For deeds I'd rather now forget.
If only one could be reborn,
And of one's guilt be truly shorn.
But there is one who does forgive,
And by whose grace rebirth can give.
Lord, grant me grace to trust in you,
And make this dream of mine come true.

Forgiveness

It haunts me still, the agony,
The recollection of that fateful day
When innocence was compromised
And I became a man of clay.

But who am I that I should doubt
The saving grace of God's own Son
To cleanse my guilt by his shed blood
And live as though the deed not done?

To arm my fight against the foe
Who whispers that "this cannot be",
The Holy Spirit makes reply,
"Trust and believe, Christ died for thee.

"And every day you serve God's will,
Forgiving others in His Name,
And share the love that he gives you,
That love will wipe away your shame."

Meditation

In still repose my soul doth find
The presence of the Lord,
For He doth come to those who seek,
And wait upon his word.

In God I trust, for by His love
And His redeeming grace,
The stresses of this earthly life
He gives me strength to face.

Within the quietness of my mind
God's still, small voice of calm
Brings order to my worldly cares
And to my soul His balm.

Love's Healing Balm

Christ is the symbol of that love
That offers what is valued most:
A life to give, and love bestow
Regardless of the heavy cost.

My sins annulled by his shed blood,
My sense of guilt and shame removed;
Grant me, O Lord, the strength to live
And love as one with life renewed.

For God is love, and love is God,
To those who show their love for Him
By loving others in His Name,
And by such love salvation bring.

PARABLES OF THE KINGDOM

The Good Neighbour

Inspired by Luke 10:25–37

The train was late and I was tired,
My shift a long one on the ward.
Off duty now, as Muslim I a Hijab wear.
A gang of drunken females, homeward bound,
Give me a stare and laughter fills the air.
At last a rumble and a rush of wind:
The last train of the night and it was full.
I stood beside a seated clergyman.
His eyes were closed. Asleep, I mused,
Or was he shutting out my world?
A Jewish boy, Hasidim by his dress,
Was also in the carriage, wrapped in prayer;
And opposite, a lad with nodding head,
A hissing sound, and wires to his ear.

At last a seat with one more stop to go.
Two men got in,
Well known on my estate
As rogues and thieves.
The iPod lad had recognized them too.
This was not good.
My body shook with fear.
It happened all so fast; a knife appeared;
A flash, a cry of pain and then they fled.
I knelt beside the lad they'd left for dead.
A nurse, I knew exactly what to do
And looked around for someone to assist:
The cleric, or perhaps Hasidic Jew;
But everyone had gone, and I was left
To staunch the bleeding wound
As best I could,
And make appeal to Allah, as one should.

The Prodigal Son

My taste of freedom was so sweet.
At last, a life to call my own.
No rules to break, for there were none,
And I could choose what's said and done.
The wine, the women, no constraint,
A life of ease, confound expense.
Until that is, I'd spent it all.
I'd squandered my inheritance.
Hard times and famine brought it home,
What I had lost, what was to come.
One thing was left: my father's love,
And pardon for a contrite son.

The Eldest Son

Relief was mine when he had gone.
My brother was no use to me.
He younger, yet my father's love
Was given in equality.
When I was told he had returned,
My heart was filled with jealousy;
My errant brother, to the fold,
It was not fair. How could this be?
For all the years I'd served him well
My father had not given me
A party, or a signet ring,
Or praise me for my loyalty.

The Father

I saw the anger in his eyes,
And this to me was no surprise;
Beloved child, could he not see
How much I prized his constancy?
When the whole world was his to roam,
He chose to stay with me at home;
Could I refuse my other son
His right of choice to have some fun?
No greater gift could I bestow
Than his free will; I let him go.
With aching heart I watched each day
For his return; for, come what may,
My love for him would never cease,
If die I must, to grant him peace.
No greater joy was mine that day
When he came home and chose to stay.

Dives and Lazarus

Inspired by Luke 16:19ff

A bowl beside him and a plea,
"Have you a coin to spare for me?"
A gentle man, he never swore;
He had his pitch beside my door.
And then I heard that he had died;
Such is the fate of all, I sighed;
Release at last from poverty,
And now he dwells in Heaven's See.
But then I also died and found
Myself in hell's deep underground.
I cried aloud to Abraham,
"Send me the beggar if you can,
To cool my tongue and whet my brow;
What use to me my riches now?"
But Abraham cried unto me,
"The gulf cannot be bridged for thee.
On earth the beggar's fate was grim
But now in heaven I comfort him.
And you, who had so much in life,
Spend all your days in pain and strife."
What of my brothers, and my worldly heirs?
"Please God let not my lot be theirs,
Could you not warn them of my fate?
Before for them it is too late."
And if one were from heaven sent,
Would they not change and sins repent?

The Sower

School was not the place for me;
I'd rather work outside.
Open fields with flocks of sheep,
And Shepherd as my guide.
He, a kind and gentle man,
Knew every flower by name,
And showed me deer and hares in spring,
That, at his bidding, came.
What he taught made sense to me:
The why, and what, and who.
This I learned from his wise lips
And thus my knowledge grew.
"See that field beyond the copse?
It's sown with winter wheat.
Seed was broadcast on the soil
That it may sprout and fruit.
Rather like that school of yours:
The teacher spreads the seed;
You're the soil that makes it grow;
And so, my lad, take heed."

The Man with Two Sons

Second thoughts are often best
When you baulk at His request.
Stubbornness of heart and mind
Never will salvation find.
There are those who say they will
But go about their business still;
Others say they won't and yet
Change of heart makes them regret.
When the Lord chose Abram's seed
They did not the prophets heed;
But to the Gentiles Christ didst come,
And children of our God become.
First be last, and last be first;
Which of these, think you, are worse?
Those God called who turned away,
Or those God's will doth now obey?

The Labourer

It's hard when you are fifty-one
And find you're out of work.
My job had seemed secure enough;
The e-mail was a shock.
They said the contracts had dried up
And I was in the cold.
A strike was called but no one cared;
The factory was sold.
I joined the firm when I left school,
And earned a decent wage.
But now I'm on the dole and broke;
They now employ by age.
My signing-in was ten to four,
The last one of the day.
The clerk looked up:
"A job for you, with pay;

"They want men up at Becket's yard.
They've got some goods to crate."
To my surprise they took me on,
Although the hour late.
At dawn, at noon, and later still,
I'd heard, the labourers came.
But when at last the job was done,
Our wages were the same.
The men who worked from dawn to dusk
Were very much aggrieved;
The hours put in were worth far more
Than what they had received.
"Your willingness to work for me,
And give your very best,
Is good enough," my master said,
"For this you will be blest."

The Useless Servant

"You're fired", he said,
With a glint in his eye.
"I gave you the means
And you did not try."
My mind went back
To the day it began.
A manager's meeting
And "executive plan".
Resources, he said,
Were on hand to expand.
And I was promoted
To be his right hand.
Well I, and two others,
Were given that day
The task of expansion
When he was away.
Buying new stock
And marketing tricks
Are all very well
If you want a quick fix.

But I'm for the long term,
The bad times to come,
Be safe, not be sorry,
When all's said and done.
The boss is a hard man
And tough as can be;
If I lose a penny,
Then woe betides me.
You'd think he'd be grateful,
But no, he was not,
For my canny prudence
He cared not a jot.
My colleagues, however,
Were praised for their zeal.
Can you imagine
How this made me feel?

The Unmercival Servant

The bank foreclosed on my estate;
I begged them for more time to pay.
A rescue plan was put in place,
And all my debt annulled that day.
My neighbour owed me fifty pounds;
It's time he cleared this paltry debt.
I took him to the small claims court.
The bailiffs came. I'd no regret.
The word was spread around that I
Had treated him so shamefully,
And shunned I was by all I met.
My point of view they could not see;
The debt he owed he must repay;
It's only fair that this should be.
For how else can you thus ensure
That you are from your debt made free?

SALVATOR MUNDI

The House at Bethany

Inspired by John 12:1–16

Of all the men that ever lived,
Would not my brother comprehend?
And see that look of coming death
Writ on the face of Christ our friend.

Did he not hear the high priest say
That one must die that all might live?
And he the sacrificial lamb;
What greater love can any give?

The fragrance of my love I'll bring
To pour upon the Saviour's feet;
A costly gesture this, I know,
But one that was both right and meet.

A token of anointing grace,
Though some may see it differently;
But Jesus knows, and scolds me not.
O Lazarus! Could they not see?

Did they not hear the words he spoke?
"Believe, and put your trust in me,
And you shall live for evermore."
O death, where is your victory?

Tomorrow we shall gather palms
To strew upon his path of pain;
And Jesus, worthy of his throne
Will tread, and thus God's Kingdom gain.

Palm Sunday

Inspired by Matthew 21:1–10

A crowd had gathered by the gate.
I watched them as they greeted him
With palms and shouts of "Here he comes,
Hosanna to the promised king."
The man upon an ass's colt
Looked up at me and caught my eye;
My pain was his, and his was mine,
For we both knew he had to die.
My role in this was to observe,
To keep the peace in Caesar's name;
But we both knew, in that one glance,
To bring God's peace was why he came.
A quiet arrest at dead of night
By soldiers of the temple guard;
A trial that mocked all decency,
And death a sentence that was marred.

I saw him next at Calvary.
The crowd who came to see him die
Looked much like those I'd seen before;
But now their cry was "Crucify!"
I cannot count myself to blame,
But yet I know within my heart
That this man's death, in all its shame,
Was cause for sorrow on my part.

The Last Supper

Both human and divine am I;
As mortal as the flesh you see.
And this, the reason I must die;
For God in man is God is me.

A cup of wine and loaf of bread:
The substance of my flesh to be
A token of the blood I shed,
And life I give, to set you free.

Remembrance is the Spirit flame
To burn eternal in your heart;
And this the reason that I came:
That I my spirit may impart.

A new commandment do I give,
To love your God, and neighbour too;
For God and I as one do live,
As I with him, and I in you.

Gethsemane

"Thy Kingdom come,
Thy will be done."
My life the fruit, and cross the press,
From which will flow the sweetest wine,

And thus, my table spread:
For cloth, my shroud;
For wine, my blood;
And bread my life endowed.

Take, eat, and drink of me.
Remember this.
The cup of love you share,
Transcends a traitor's kiss.

To you and all the world,
Myself I give
In sacrifice,
That I in you might live.

Good Friday

Inspired by Luke 23:22–47

He spoke to me of paradise,
A place I'd rather be
Than on this cross of shame and pain,
For all the world to see.
What justice was there in his death?
In spite of what they claim,
A man may think himself a king,
But acts fulfil the name.
For my own part I thought the world
Was there for me to take,
A place to ravage and to steal,
And my own kingdom make.
They decked him in a purple robe,
A crown upon his head,
And nailed a sign above the cross,
"The King of Jews" it read.

In spite of all they did to him,
"Forgive them, Lord" he cried.
And this the man a kiss betrayed,
And whom his friends denied.
"Have you no fear of God?" I said,
In answer to their cry;
"If you are truly God's own son
Then save us ere we die."
Remember me, O Lord, I pray,
And all my sins forgive
That I might be at one with you
And in your presence live.
Then darkness fell upon the earth,
"Come, follow me," he cried.
And heaven's portal opened wide,
When on the cross Christ died.

Crucifixion

*Inspired by the Crucifixion sculpture in
St Asaph Cathedral, North Wales*

A naked form with tortured limbs,
At point of death and agony,
A corpse, of rotting flesh and bone—
A symbol of mortality.

But gaze upon this cross of shame
With inward eye, and you will see
The sinfulness of humankind
Cleansed by Christ's blood upon this tree.

And this the place of death, and birth,
A fulcrum for God's true intent
To bring new life and future hope
To all who of their sins repent.

Sabbath Calm

Shone no more the Saviour's light,
That which shone ere world began.
Came the darkness of the night,
Ere God's Word created man.

By his death, the blood Christ shed,
Substance gave to earth below.
Grape for wine and wheat for bread,
Seed God's Son for us didst sow.

Rock-hewn cave, an empty tomb,
Sabbath calm: God's work was done.
Sunrise for a world new born;
Come the dawn, new life begun.

Easter Dawn

In a cave they laid our Saviour
Who, for us, was crucified.
Sorrow filled the heart of Mary
On that Friday when Christ died.
Weep not, Mary, for our Saviour,
From the grave he will arise,
For he lives within your heart still
With a love that never dies.

His the death for your tomorrow,
Hope, the sunrise that is nigh
When you see the new dawn breaking,
Gone the dark clouds in the sky.
Comfortless he will not leave you,
This the promise he has made;
When you need him most he'll be there,
Christ our Saviour by your side.

We the cave of Christ's indwelling,
He in us let others see.
Let our lives show forth his presence;
From the grave bring victory.
Born again and sins forgiven,
Cleansed by his redeeming blood,
Strengthened by the Holy Spirit,
We proclaim His living word.

Snowdrops in a Country Churchyard

Grey monoliths of slate and stone,
Give name to ancient flesh and bone,
Who, but for this, would be forgot:
Their winter come, they lie and rot.

But nature's mantle, virgin snow,
A blanket forms for bulbs below.
Which now await the sun to bring
The promise of new life, come spring.

Up-thrusting from the soil beneath
To crown the Easter dawn,
The snowdrop casts aside her shroud
And greets God's Son and is reborn.

Thomas

How blessed are we who have not seen,
Yet in our hearts believe.
Our faith in Christ will give us sight
His presence to perceive.

Of human flesh was Jesus made,
And suffered for our sin.
He rose again in human form,
That we might rise with him.

Upon the cross Christ bore our pain
Whose wounds are with us still;
The hurt and hunger of our world,
He calls us now to heal.

How blest are we who see him now
In every needful face
And every act of love outpoured
In token of God's grace.

TRANSFORMING GRACE

Bible Sunday

Inspired by Luke 1:1–4.

There is one in the house, I think,
A bible from my days at school,
We had to read it then, of course,
For Holy Scripture was the rule.

I cannot say I've read it since;
For me it had no relevance;
And God a word I used in oath
Not one I used in penitence.

But with the onset of old age,
Its stories now I do recall:
The promise of eternal life,
And God's abiding love for all.

It comforts me to dwell on this,
The things that Jesus said and did;
And with the passing of the years
Their meaning is no longer hid.

They say that wisdom grows with age
And nothing new is ever done,
For life is much the same today,
As once it was when life began.

The stories that the Saviour told,
The way he gave his life to save:
All this I learned when I was young,
And these I'll take unto my grave.

A Grain of Sand

Inspired by Genesis 22:17–18

As I stood on a lonely shore,
I thought of all the human race,
Both now, the future, and before,
Created by God's loving grace.

The Lord with blessing did behest
To Abraham a promised land,
From north and south and east and west,
And children, numberless as sand.

One grain I am, so vast a host;
Can God have any thought for me?
There's no achievement I can boast,
No grand estate, or high degree.

But in the stillness of my heart,
The awesome truth at last I see,
That God in Christ is calling me
His presence in this world to be.

Christian Hope

Inspired by Genesis 1:24–2:3

The world that God has made for me,
Each forest, glade, and branch of tree,
Each meadow and each blade of grass:
Can I ensure this does not pass?
Creation's gift to me God gave.
But have I strength his world to save?
I look around me with despair.
It seems the world has ceased to care.
No longer are our churches full;
It seems the world has lost its soul.
The good for man that God has willed
Has by man's greed been unfulfilled,
But God who made the world and me
Gave also of His Son to be
Our strength, our guide, and saving grace,
And show to man God's human face.

The Evil Within

Inspired by 1 Peter 5:8–11

Can God and Satan co-exist,
Or was creation made amiss?
The good we would, we cannot do,
Without the good Christ gives to you.

Opposing armies, good and ill,
Do struggle for the human will;
But by God's grace is battle won,
And Satan vanquished by His Son;

Yet not without due sacrifice;
His life he gave, and this the price.
To overcome the sin within,
We too must give our lives to Him.

Hear My Voice

Inspired by John 10:15–16

I heard a voice that called my name,
A voice from deep within,
"I gave my life that you might live
Forever freed from sin."
The weight of guilt I'd born so long
Was lifted from my mind;
And now I longed to spread the word
That others, too, might find
Assurance of God's saving grace
To all who heed His call,
And put their trust in Christ Our Lord
Who died to save us all.

Resolution (New Year's Day)

Haunted by the memory
Of past endeavours to be good,
I wonder if perchance this year
With guiding hand, I really could.

Deciding what was right and wrong
Were met by arguments so strong:
Persuasive in their subtlety,
Convinced was I that right was wrong.

But conscience tells me otherwise,
And guilt now rears its ugly head;
So try I must this coming year
To lead the life that Jesus led.

The human heart is the life force of our being. Jesus refers to the activity of the human heart in terms of responsive activity, and in the Gospels the most notable references are to purity, meekness, goodness, uprightness, belief, steadfastness, and understanding. The heart is predominantly associated with love, and as such it is universally linked with the expressive display of human affection and regard for another.

Blessed are the pure in heart,
for they will see God.

Matthew 5:8

"On that day you will realize that I am in my Father, and you are in me, and I am in you. Whoever has my commands and keeps them is the one who loves me. The one who loves me will be loved by my Father, and I too will love them and show myself to them."

Then Judas (not Judas Iscariot) said, "But, Lord, why do you intend to show yourself to us and not to the world?"

Jesus replied, "Anyone who loves me will obey my teaching. My Father will love them, and we will come to them and make our home with them. Anyone who does not love me will not obey my teaching. These words you hear are not my own; they belong to the Father who sent me.

"All this I have spoken while still with you. But the Advocate, the Holy Spirit, whom the Father will send in my name, will teach you all things and will remind you of everything I have said to you. Peace I leave with you; my peace I give you. I do not give to you as the world gives. Do not let your hearts be troubled and do not be afraid."

John 14:20–27

Divine Love

Inspired by 1 Corinthians 13

A word,
A touch,
A promise to fulfil;
A union of heart
And mind, and will;
An ache, a yearning,
And a cross to bear;
A sacrificial act;
Self-giving.
And a life
To share.

Eidolon

Earthbound shadow
On the ground,
Eidolon that
Makes no sound;
Let your spirit
Share my space,
Sacred make,
By Godly grace.
Consubstantial
Presence be,
Light from darkness
Make of me.

Eidolon is an image or spectre. It can also be used, as in "eidouranion", to describe a mechanical device for representing the motions of the heavenly bodies.

THE LORD IS HERE

The Lord Is Here

We preach of heaven up above
And Christ enthroned as king on high.
But is this truly why he came
As man to suffer and to die?

The here and now is God's abode,
For did not Christ a promise give,
That he would always with us be?
And this the truth we must believe.

"The Lord is here," at mass we say,
As we partake of bread and wine,
For with us does His Spirit dwell,
And we His living word and sign.

Christ died for us that he might live
Not up above, but here on earth
Within the hearts and minds of all
Who give themselves to his new birth.

The Pelican

The books I read when I was young
Made much of those prepared to fight;
To rescue damsels in distress,
And stand their ground for what is right.
A war child like myself thought this
A noble and a goodly thing:
To risk one's life to save the world
For God, our country, and our King.
I think of stories I was told,
Of men like Oates, of Polar fame,
Who put the needs of others first
Without a thought for praise or gain;
And then there is the pelican
Who plucked her breast to feed her brood
(Our lectern in the village church,
Symbolic of Christ's out-poured blood).

Midnight Mass

On Christmas Eve the Square was full:
The music, lights, and place to be;
But few had chosen to attend
The feast of "Christ's Nativity".

As midnight struck I raised the Host,
And from outside a distant cheer;
The Church, the World, and I were one;
The Babe of Bethlehem was here.

It mattered not, the empty pews,
And numbers in the church but small:
The Prince of Peace was come to bring
Salvation and new birth to all.

The city streets are empty now.
The crowds have gone, and all is still,
Save for the echo of my steps,
And laughter from an all-night grill.

Corpus Christi

One with God in humankind,
One with God in heart and mind,
One with God in word and deed,
One with God for those in need,
One with God his cross to bear,
One with God his love to share,
One with God his will be mine,
One with God, in bread, and wine.

Heaven's Gate

Inspired by Ephesians 1:9–10

A whisper that becomes a roar:
Does God exist? And is there more
To life than just a measured beat,
The will to live, and dawn to greet?

Relentless are the passing years;
And at the end, a mourner's tears.
Hope springs eternal, so they say;
And we shall see another day.

But is there yet another plane?
A hallowed realm that has no pain;
An Erewhon or Shangri-La
That shines above us as a star?

I look beyond the clouds to see
If I can glimpse eternity.
But God's abode is not therein;
To seek it one should look within.

Eternity

Inspired by Revelation 21:1-7

My death is but a passing cloud,
A shadow that obscures the sun;
For life is hid within the soul
That never dies but still lives on.

For God is that eternal love
That dwells within the human heart,
Uniting me with God himself
When I this earthly life depart.

For all that is of God lives on;
And all that is of God in me
Is one with Christ, God's Risen Son,
And lives for all eternity.

Agnus Dei

The husbandry of all God's gifts
And nature of all being one,
The chain of death that leads to life,
And sacrifice of God's own Son.

I looked for answer to the fields
Where cattle graze and lambs do play,
And thought upon their future plight,
For human need, the price they pay.

The shrew caught by a coursing owl
With hungry chicks to feed:
Would that it knew his death gave life
To other creatures in their need.

My earthly frame Christ's body be,
To house the wondrous mystery
Of bread become his sacred flesh,
That he might be reborn in me.

Emmanuel

Is not the Son at one with man?
And was this not so
Since the world began?
For the life we must live
Is the love that we give;
And the love that we give
Is that Christ may live.

ALL GOD'S CREATURES

In the "Laudes Creaturarum", the Canticle of the Sun, written in about 1224, St Francis gives expression to his belief in the unity of all created being, referring to animals as brothers and sisters to mankind. It has been the custom in many parishes to have a service of blessing for animals, giving thanks to God for the love and devotion of our pets and the importance of animal husbandry and the duty of care placed upon us by God for all that he has created. I wrote the following poems for the services on Christmas Eve to convey in a simple way the message of God's infinite and universal love. Christ's birth in a stable conveys a depth of meaning that never ceases to inspire us with wonder and awe, with its evocation of sight, smell, and warming breath of livestock. Truly, God is here, in our midst, in stable yard and stately mansion, and in all that is and ever was.

O Magnum Mysterium

Gathered round the Holy Child,
All creation, tame and wild,
Flora, Fauna, child of Eve,
God incarnate to perceive.

His the breath of man and beast,
Breath of God, for great and least,
Natal cry at each new birth,
God at one with all on earth.

Jenny's Christmas

The air was crisp with a hint of snow,
And Jenny the donkey paced to and fro,
Waiting for someone to open the door,
And spread out her hay on the stable floor.

Inside the cave it was warm and dry,
And Jenny the donkey let out a sigh.
"I pity the people with nowhere to stay;
The inn is quite full and they've turned folks away".

At dead of night the door was untied
And Mary and Joseph were ushered inside.
Awakened, she gazed at the baby who lay
Asleep in a manger—on her precious hay!

Jenny was angry. "How dare they do this!"
But when she saw Mary give Jesus a kiss,
The anger she felt was soon turned to shame,
For love is to give, and receive in God's name.

The Christmas Mouse

At the inn they were full,
No room could be found
For Mary and Joseph,
Bethlehem bound.
It was cold outside
And beginning to snow;
Surely there's somewhere
That they could go?

A mouse popped up
From a hole in the floor,
And gazed at the couple
Who entered the door;
They are welcome to stay
In my stable, thought he.
There's plenty of room
For a mother-to-be.

The field mice, who lived
With the shepherds, had said
They'd seen a bright star,
And the news had spread
That this very night
A king would be born
In Bethlehem town,
Before the new dawn.

But would the Messiah
The prophets foretold,
Be born in a stable?
Yet, lo and behold!
Wonder of wonders,
A son by God's grace
Was given to Mary
In that humble place.

The mouse, as silent
As mice can be,
Crept to the manger
And peered in to see;
Could this little baby
Be really a king?
He looked so tiny, so
Fragile a thing.

The babe in the manger,
Looked—to his eyes—
Like all other babies,
And this no surprise,
For God in his image
Made all humankind,
And asks all his children to
Bear this in mind.

The Shepherd's Dog

My master on that Christmas Eve,
Sent me to guard his sheep.
He knew he could rely on me
A watchful eye to keep.

I sniffed the air for scent of foe,
And pricked my ears for sound,
But, just in case, though all seemed well,
I made another round.

The city was in darkness now
And all seemed quiet within;
The couple who had asked the way,
I hope had found their inn.

The eastern sky, ablaze with light
Lit up the shepherds field,
And suddenly, before my eyes,
God's messenger appeared.

"Fear not," he said, "I bring good news,
This night in David's town
The Saviour of the World is born,
And God to earth come down.

"And this the sign, a babe you'll find,"
The blessed angel said,
"All tightly wrapped in swaddling clothes,
And in a manger laid."

The air was filled with sound of praise,
As heaven's host did sing,
"All glory be to God on high
For peace on earth we bring."

My master's sheep I knew were safe
From predatory harm;
For I recalled what had been writ,
That wolf would lie with lamb.

In haste my master journeyed forth
To seek the holy child,
But did he know precisely where?
And to his aid I hied.

Just as I thought, my master had
Assumed it was the inn,
But I knew best and barked at him
And nipped him on the shin.

The mention of a manger was
The clue that came to mind,
And where but in a stable would
The holy child be found?

He knew my ways and followed me
As to the stable door
I led my master, to the babe,
Asleep on bed of straw.

The Christmas Lamb

Below the town of Bethlehem
The shepherd grazed his flock.
The hillside steep and treacherous,
With boulders, scree, and rock.

His ewes were drawing near the time
When they would bring forth young,
And needed extra nourishment
For strength of heart and lung.

The weather broke on Christmas Eve,
And rain had turned to snow;
Deep drifts had formed upon the hills.
His sheep to fold must go.

But for one ewe her time had come.
And, sheltered from the storm,
Beneath a limestone overhang,
Her little lamb was born.

The shepherd counted one by one
His sheep into the fold,
But where the little newborn lamb?
Lost, frightened, wet, and cold.

Though late the hour he journeyed forth
Into the bitter night
To seek the errant little lamb;
No thought for his own plight.

Pitch black the night, and hard to see,
And treacherous the way;
But steadfastly he climbed the hill
In search of waif and stray.

And there before him was the lamb
Illum'd in heaven's rays,
And angel voices from above
Sang God's Almighty praise.

"Be not afraid," the angels said,
"For joyful news we bring:
The coming of the promised one,
God's Son, the Shepherd King."

At bidding of the angel host,
In haste the shepherd went
To Bethlehem to see the babe,
The lamb from heaven sent.

And at the feet of Mary's child,
Upon this hallowed ground
The shepherd placed his little lamb,
That by God's light was found.

The Lamb of God salvation brought
To earth from heaven above,
That lost souls be for evermore
Enfolded by God's love.

The Coming

The night was cold
And pavement hard.
Sacking for blanket
And mattress of card.

The streets were thronged
With people intent
On getting their presents
And Christmas cards sent.

A coin or two thrown into my cap
But never a smile, never a glance,
Too frightened to look
At their own fate, perchance.

A rich man, now poor,
A beggar, not thief;
How easy to label
A man in his grief.

I thought of the good times,
When all was well,
'Till the stress and the drink
Turned my life into hell.

And then all was quiet,
The last tram had gone;
Alone in my doorway
I thought of God's Son.

We had much in common,
The Christ-child and me:
An outhouse, a stable,
No fit place to be.

At midnight I woke,
When a voice in my ear
Roused me from sleep
And bade me good cheer.

A sandwich and soup,
A welcoming face,
The world seemed much brighter
When lit by God's grace.

What greater joy
Could there ever be
Than love given freely
In God's name to me.

Epilogue

My journey of faith has taken me to the depths of despair and to the heights of heaven. I have been privileged to serve the Lord in many beautiful places, and have shared the joy of birth, the despair of those in prison, the grief of the bereaved, and, as a father, the excitement of children in their exploration of the wonders of the world around them. But my greatest joy has been to witness the power of unselfish love to transform the lives of others, be it the giving of aid and support to the needy, the homeless, the refugee; or a helping hand to an elderly neighbour. God is love, and no greater love can we give than of ourselves to others in the name of Jesus Christ who gave of himself for us.

> Lord, grant me eyes to see as thee;
> The faith to know the "thee" in me;
> The strength to act as thou wouldst do;
> And will to live my life for you.

Lightning Source UK Ltd.
Milton Keynes UK
UKHW02f1447090118
315826UK00005B/96/P